LONDON TRANSPORT BUSES IN EAST LONDON AND ESSEX

THE 1960S AND 1970S

David Christie

AMBERLEY

First published 2017

Amberley Publishing
The Hill, Stroud
Gloucestershire, GL5 4EP

www.amberley-books.com

Copyright © David Christie, 2017

The right of David Christie to be identified as
the Author of this work has been asserted in
accordance with the Copyrights, Designs and
Patents Act 1988.

ISBN 978 1 4456 6800 0 (print)
ISBN 978 1 4456 6801 7 (ebook)

British Library Cataloguing in Publication Data.
A catalogue record for this book is available from
the British Library.

Origination by Amberley Publishing.
Printed in the UK.

Introduction

Born in 1943, the author went through the normal (in those days) hobby of collecting numbers, not only of buses but also trains. This eventually led to photography in 1962, when I purchased my first camera, a Petri 7, for capturing in colour the remaining steam on BR. It wasn't until 1967 that I realised I should be doing likewise for buses, prompted by discovering Routemasters being used on Sunday workings on my local 86 route. This, I thought, was the end of the RT, not realising that they would still be found working some ten years hence!

Romford was my home town; it was a very different place in my youth, having a cattle market in its centre for instance and a large brewery in which my father worked. We lived just a few hundred yards from London Road at Crowlands, one mile east of the town centre. Our local bus route, the 86 or 86A into town, used Utility Arabs when I was in short trousers and I well remember being informed by my mother when one of these arrived at the bus stop that if the engine bonnet side was open it would be one or other of these routes (one route turned right at the town centre for Upminster, whereas the other went straight on to Brentwood). As the Guys invariably seemed to need extra engine cooling, this was not exactly good thinking! However, Romford was awash with Guys until the new RT took over, which then predominated, with the odd route using RTLs, and two single-decker routes using TDs. We were also well situated for a mile-long bus ride in the opposite direction to Chadwell Heath, where London trolleybuses could be seen at their eastern-most terminus. If funds allowed, a longer ride was undertaken by Green Line route 721 to Aldgate, which was usually combined with nearby Liverpool Street station to provide a heady mix of steam, trolleys and buses. Alas, the trolleys went in 1962, just before I started photography of any kind, so I was too late, with only the wiring standards remaining, in some places for some years, to be recorded in my shots.

So, 1967 was the beginning as far as bus photography went, with the purchase of a car in the same year helping in this respect. Working locally I was able to run around before or after work to capture various routes. All this came to a sudden halt in February 1973 when moving house to Scotland with my parents meant that LT coverage from then on became a possibility only on a few trips back down south.

This book begins in Aldgate bus and Green Line terminus, before heading east to Stepney and taking a dive south by the docks before coming back up to Poplar, with RTLs well in evidence. Going a short distance north to Bromley-by-Bow, the single deck RF-worked 208 route towards Hackney is followed, to pick up on the lowbridge RLH-worked 178. The two routes are combined at Clapton terminus. The 178 route then heads back to Stratford, where it mingled with RTLs, RTs and Green Line coaches, including RFs. Stratford was another of my favourite childhood spots with its trolleys on the cobbles, probably the same remaining in my RTL shots here. A few odd shots follow before Barking is reached, with its very open garage area – so easy to photograph. Ilford is next – surprisingly short on visits – before Becontree Heath terminus with its furthest worked RTLs. Chadwell Heath marks the end (in my view) of London. We then take a turn northwards up to Hainault and Lambourne End, arriving way up in Epping before coming back down to the western outskirts of Romford.

Romford is approached via London Road past my local stop and into the centre traffic lights crossroads. The Market Place and North Street are shown before reaching Romford station via South Street. Onwards, we turn down Oldchurch Road a short way for the Green Line 722, then to Roneo Corner where we come back in a circle via Junction Road – a diversion route while the ring road was being constructed. Being at the eastern end of the Market, we follow Main Road towards Gidea Park. Hornchurch is then visited with the far south east terminus of the red central routes at Rainham.

Then it is back up to Harold Hill before reaching Upminster with its RLHs on route 248. These were a favourite of mine, and are well covered! Corbets Tey terminus also has Green Line interest before we finish up in Brentwood. I used to change vehicles here in the late 1950s when visiting my newly married sister in Rayleigh. The change from a fast Green Line RT to a lumbering Eastern National Lodekka was quite a shock – especially as the Lodekka was a newer design! It really showed that the LT design was in a different class.

All the images are mine own, mostly taken with my Petri but some with my first SLR, a Minolta SRT101 purchased in 1971. Film used was invariably Agfa CT18 at speed 50asa.

Vehicle details

RT – Some 4,800 were built from 1947–1954 and were AEC Regent Mk III, mainly bodied by Park Royal and Weymann, with a small number by Saunders and Craven. The chassis and body on most were interchangeable, so that one never knew the exact chassis and body detail from the fleet number. The Craven bodies were really different, with extra windows and a more upright profile –being non-standard, these were sold off early.

RTL – These had the same bodies and dates as the RTs, but had Leyland PD2 chassis, with only 1,630 being built. Metro-Cammell built 450 of these, and they are easily identified by their reduced depth cantrail relief. Like the Cravens RTs, these were among the first to be withdrawn.

RTW – A 500-strong class, all of which were 1949-built Leylands with 8-foot-wide Leyland bodies.

RLH – These were standard provincial AEC Regents with a taller radiator than the RT and completely different lowbridge Weymann bodywork. Only seventy-six were put into service, in two batches in 1950 and 1952.

RM – The Routemaster was designed in 1954 but production did not start until 1959. These were AEC or Leyland engined with Park Royal integral bodies. Some 2,120 were built with an additional sixty-eight coach versions built in 1962 and designated as RMC. Production changed in 1965 to the longer 30-foot RML version (a small batch were previously built in 1961) with over 500 built, the coach version numbering 43 and being designated as RCL.

RF – The standard single-decker built from 1951–1953 was an AEC Regal Mk IV, underfloor-engined with Metro-Cammell bodywork. Some 700 were built. During 1967 some were modernised with twin headlights, curved windscreen and fluorescent lighting. They were also given a smart two-tone livery with a broad pale-green band.

Aldgate

RT1167 arrives at the terminus on the 23 route, pictured on 8 September 1967. The 23 route started to gain RMs in November 1959 but was not totally converted.

RTL1465 awaits its next turn on the 25. This route, worked by RTLs until the end of the class in late 1968, became RT operated for a few years, before RMs took over in January 1972. Taken on 8 September 1967.

Green Line RT610 arrives on 8 September 1967 on the 722 route, passing RTL1465. The 722 route, unlike its big brother the 721, never went over to RCLs, being a 'rush-hour' route that was withdrawn in August 1968.

Aldgate was a favourite turning place for learners and here is RTW410 from Seven Kings garage, pictured on 8 September 1967. The RTWs started to be displaced from their routes in 1966, some becoming trainers for a few years until 1970, when learning duties were taken over by RTs.

Romford RE garage's Green Line coaches always added a touch of class at Aldgate, being kept in immaculate condition. Here is RT999, photographed on 8 September 1967 and ready for service on the 722. Nine RTs were kept at RE for this route.

RT999 again, showing the newly applied 'Jessups' advert on the rear. Green Line vehicles normally carried no advertising. The blinds, set to 'Private', would soon be changed as per the previous page. Pictured here on 8 September 1967.

Seven years on from the first image in this book, on 7 May 1974, RM10 is the normal type on the 23 route. Also seen here are two Green Line vehicles, an all-over advert RP type on the 720 and a LN on the 721. The RP was an AEC Reliance coach that replaced the double-deck RCL on many Green Line routes; it in turn was supplanted by the LN Leyland National bus.

RT3635 arrives on the 722, the destination blind already having been changed. A RML bus is parked at the bus station entrance. Photographed on 6 November 1967.

RTL504 pulls away from Aldgate tube station on the 10, pictured on 8 September 1967. This route became RT operated when the RTLs were all withdrawn in late 1968, until October 1972 when the DMS class took over.

Stepney

A Sunday working on the 9 route, RT4341 heads back to Barking garage on 25 February 1968. This route was normally RM worked but both RTs and RTLs were to be seen at times.

Limehouse

RTL1304 is pictured on 7 November 1967, on its way to tour the Isle of Dogs on route 277.

Cubitt Town

RTL145 turns at the terminus of the 277, just by the West India Docks lifting bridge, on 7 November 1967. This route, after the RTLs went in late 1968, for part of its length went over to RTs, a narrow bridge preventing anything wider. DMS types took over the rest, and then the whole route in 1976.

Blackwall Tunnel

RTL384 emerges at the south end of the new tunnel on 7 November 1967, which was only completed six months previously. This RTL was one of twenty-three fitted with an early 'roof route box' body in 1964. Route 108 became the province of new MB buses from October 1968, when the RTLs were withdrawn.

Poplar

RTL88 is photographed on 7 November 1967 in a traditional East End scene passing a corner shop on its way to Blackwall tunnel on route 108. The ornate lamppost is remarkable.

Poplar Garage

RTLs galore on 25 February 1968, with RTL1457 showing route 56. The RTLs were all gone from Poplar garage just six months later, and route 56 went in October 1969, replaced by the 277.

A broadside view of RTL1457. Pictured on 25 February 1968.

In the depths of the garage on 25 February 1968 was trainer RTW250.

Bow Church

The new regime for trainers, with RT3739 passing Bow Church on 27 March 1970.

Near Bow

A surprisingly empty main road with a very clean RT1145 stopping on the 25 route. Note the un-blanked radiator, giving the bus a 'new' look. Pictured on 19 April 1969.

Bromley-by-Bow

'Top-Box' RTL1438 at the 108 route terminus on 7 November 1967.

RF493 turning at the 208 terminus on 27 March 1970 in the last few weeks of RF operation before MBS buses took over in April.

Old Ford

The 208 was a rare example of East London RF operation using vehicles without doors. RF395 is shown on 27 March 1970 at the Tredegar Road railway bridge, one of the few locally where the railway passed under the road.

RF467 is seen, again on 27 March 1970, with the more normal arrangement of multiple railway bridges over the road.

Hackney Wick

RLH58 turns sharply at the Lord Napier Inn on the 178, the only East London route to use lowbridge RLHs. Twelve of the class were allocated to Dalston garage for the route. Pictured on 22 July 1967.

RLH49 is seen from the other direction; it is another recently repainted bus, surprisingly with cream relief rather than the current dove grey. Also photographed on 22 July 1967.

Clapton Pond

Both 'odd' routes, the 208 and 178 ended up at Clapton Pond; here are RLH58 and RF394 at the terminus on 8 July 1967.

RF394 at Clapton on 8 July 1967.

RLH54 and RLH56 at the terminus; the high seating on the top deck is noticeable in this shot taken on 6 November 1967.

A full house at the Pond with two RLHs and three RFs on 28 March 1970.

The last week of RLH operation on the 178, and also the last RLH route with a dishevelled RLH58 at the terminus on 10 April 1971.

Stratford Carpenters Road
RLH64 crosses over the Canal bridge on 27 March 1971.

RLH61 passes the Carpenters Arms and huge blocks of flats, which were presumably why double-deckers were needed on this route. Photographed on 10 April 1971.

Stratford Broadway

RTL1283 arrives on the granite setts on route 10. Where the RM is parked, some seven years previous there would have been trolleybuses all in a line. Pictured on 22 July 1967.

A trolley standard remains in this view of RTL388 on route 25. This RTL seems to have acquired unusually large headlights. Photographed on 22 July 1967.

On another route 25, 'Top Box' RTL1383 turns east from Broadway on 22 July 1967.

Lowbridge RLH67 arrives on route 178, closely followed by a '25' RTL on 22 July 1967. Parked by the church is my first car, a Hillman Imp Californian – all of one month old.

Four years on and the 25 route is worked by RTs, but only for eight more months before the all-conquering RMs took over. Here is RT4421 being overtaken by modified RF155 on Green Line route 720. The RFs on this route were replaced in March 1973 by RPs displaced from the 721 service. Photographed on 10 April 1971.

RTL1360 on route 10. A shop that was everywhere at the time can be seen in the distance but Fine Fare would disappear twenty years later as a trading name. Pictured on 7 November 1967.

Trainer RTW44 appears at the same spot, also on 7 November 1967, where a comparison can be made with the previous picture showing the RTWs extra six inches width. The advertising on this bus seems big on Distillers Co. products, being the company I went to work for in 1973 until retiral (then Diageo) in 2004.

RMC1495 on the 721 route, an unusual sight on 10 April 1971, as this route used RCLs exclusively on its full service. RMCs were used at this time on the 723, operating from Grays garage, which had cut back some of its services; presumably a few of their vehicles found their way to Romford RE garage, which operated the 721.

RLH61 in a general scene at the Broadway, with an RT type and trolley standards well in evidence on 10 April 1971.

RLH53 passes a request stop attached to an old trolley standard, easily identified from its extra girth and a distinct lean-back. Pictured on 27 March 1971.

Maryland

RLH61 leaves the 178 terminus as the conductor changes the front destination blind. The once-smart condition of these buses from a few years back has deteriorated, but then this was 10 April 1971, their last week in service.

Pulling away from the terminus a year earlier, on 28 March 1970, is RLH57. The front route blind has confusingly lost the first digit of its route number 178.

Forest Gate

One of my RM shots, rarely photographed at the time. Newly out-shopped RM160 turns at the crossroads on route 58, passing not only ex-trolley standards but also BR ER dark-blue signs. The RMs on this route lasted until the early 1980s. Photographed on 27 March 1970.

Wanstead

RT2134 on learner duties, pictured on 27 March 1970. This was the period, from 1969 to June 1970, during which the RTW trainers were replaced by RTs. Presumably this was in the name of standardisation on AECs but, from thereon, the drivers just had to imagine that they were learning on 8-foot-plus-wide vehicles!

North Woolwich Ferry

RM56 arrives on the 69 on 25 February 1972. This was one of my childhood haunts, with trolleybuses on the 669 terminating here to turn right across the road. The trolley standards remain in this shot, which is the only one taken here due to my (at the time) reluctance to photograph RMs. OMO happened on this route in the mid-1980s.

Barking Garage

This was a great place for easy access to the buses kept in the open. Here, on 25 February 1968, are three of the RTW trainers, RTW 46, 69 and 407, still looking reasonably smart; a nice touch, when being repainted for their new role, was the application of the earlier cream relief band.

A RF interloper (RF495) amid the RTs (RT4272, 2221 and 2811) on 25 February 1968. Route 23C was withdrawn in March 1973, while the 169A and 179 went over to OMO operation in July 1971 and September 1973 respectively.

Three RTs (RT3830, 2441 and 2198) and five RTWs line up on 25 February 1968. The nearest RTWs are the ones in the first picture shown here, in addition to an unidentified pair. The different styles of headlamps are noticeable.

Another line-up, but this time of storage buses out of use on 11 April 1970. RTs 4608, 3787 and 1169 appear with RM292 (presumably not for sale) and four RTWs, which have finished their days as trainers.

Ilford Crossroads

Taken on 7 May 1974 on one of my visits south from Scotland, RT2568, on the 86 route at the crossroads, passes a United Dairies lorry loaded with milk crates containing bottles – a sight no more to be seen. The 86 route, being my local, features further on in this book.

Ilford Cranbrook Road

On local route 129, RT2565 is in Cranbrook Road on 7 May 1974. This route went over to OMO in October 1976.

Ilford Station

RT1369 passes the station on the 150 on 7 May 1974. The slip board states 'To and from Hainault Forest'. The route went to OMO in 1977.

Becontree Heath

RT4378 passes close to the terminal here on the 175, the RTs on this route being replaced by RMs in 1977 and these by Titans in 1982. The block capital main blind seen on RT4378 continued to be used at some garages well after the lower case was introduced in 1961. Pictured on 17 March 1968.

At the terminal on 6 May 1967 with a view looking across RTL437, which is on the 25 route, to RT1912 on the 87. The 87 route was one of the last to be operated by RTs in 1979.

RTL315 at the terminal on 6 May 1967 showing a short working on route 25.

'Top Box' RT1132 leaves on a Sunday working on route 9 on 17 March 1968.

RTL388 leaves on the full working of route 25 on 3 September 1967, showing another old capital blind.

RT43777 on a Sunday 9 working, which was normally undertaken by RMs. The use of RTs on Sundays ceased in September 1968. Pictured on 3 September 1967.

Goodmayes

Freshly overhauled RT1196 looks in fine fettle on the 86 route, the only blemish being the mucky radiator badge and, of course, the lack of rear wheel discs, all having been removed five months previously. I often wonder what became of them! Photographed on 13 April 1972.

Chadwell Heath

My first ever bus photograph, taken on 6 May 1967, of RT4313 turning on a short working of the 86 route. My local route, the 86, started to gain RMs from February 1976 and went OMO in 1985. Chadwell Heath was the eastern-most trolley terminal and was just a short bus ride on the 86 from home, so I spent a lot of time there as a lad.

RT1614 on route 62 heads for the station on 17 April 1972. This narrow stretch of road over the railway was the reason the RTs lasted so long, as to use wider buses would have been unsafe. This was the last RT route, the last day being 7 April 1979. A trolley standard on the turn in Wangye Road is still standing.

Whalebone Lane

A short way east of Chadwell Heath, the 139 route turned north up to Eastern Avenue, the A12 road. Coming off the roundabout here is RT3695 heading south. This route lost its RTs in July 1977 and was finally withdrawn ten years later. Pictured on 5 April 1969.

Marks Gate

RT1123, on a cold Sunday 30 January 1972, is on route 62 with no passengers.

Hainault Hog Hill

Famed for being the only hill of any size around Romford, Hog Hill was on the 62 route and here is RT2796 breasting the hill on 3 June 1971.

RT2796 heads south off the hill on 3 June 1971.

Lambourne End, The Maypole
Route 150A terminated here at the Maypole Inn. Here are RTs 720 and 2177 on 27 March 1970. From 1977 this route terminated at Chigwell Row.

Bournebridge

An unusually rural setting for a LT red bus, 'top-box' RT3686 pulls away from the request stop on 12 October 1968, having just dropped off two passengers. Route 175 at its longest ran right out to Ongar, a real outpost for the red central routes. The 'top-box' RTs were phased out by June 1970.

At the same stop, RF444 runs past on the 250 route, bound for Epping on 12 October 1968.

Stapleford Abbotts
RT2719, pictured in the low winter sunshine on 3 January 1970, passes an old wooden signpost on route 175.

Epping Green
RF440 turns at the terminus of the 250 route on 27 March 1970.

RF440 at the 250 terminus on 27 March 1970. The RFs were replaced by BLs in April 1976 but the route itself was withdrawn in January 1977, being replaced by a revised 247.

Romford London Road

RT4331 on the 86 routes crosses the 'Cabbage Patch', which is what we called the farmland strip separating Romford from Chadwell Heath (and London!). Route 86 was converted to OMO in 1985. Photographed on 5 April 1969.

A mix of vehicles here with RT2642 on route 193, passing RCL2223 on the 721, with the following Green Line RT3438 showing 'Private' blinds. The 193 route went to RMs in 1977 and then to OMO in 1982. Photograph taken at Southern Way, on 6 May 1967.

Romford Crowlands

RT3566 on route 86 passes The Crown pub and also my junior school, before pulling into my local stop for London. Pictured on 5 April 1969.

RT2285 leaves my local stop amid the snows of 1969 for the town centre on route 86. The street with the bungalows beside The Crown is Spring Gardens, which ran into Jubilee Avenue, where I used to live. The car park, being the snow-covered area, was for Romford Stadium, a Greyhound track situated on the opposite side of London Road. Photograph taken on 8 February 1969.

RT929 approaches 'my' stop on the 193 route, bound for Barking on 5 April 1969.

Romford RE London Road Garage

This was the Green Line garage just half a mile from my home, which was responsible primarily for the main 721 service and also the 722. Here RT3635 leaves to take up the 722 route, while modified RF110 is set up for the 724 – a new route started in July 1966. Pictured on 18 May 1967.

A rare shot of the blinds set for the 721 on an RT, a familiar sight pre-1965, which is when RCLs took over this route. RT3438 arrives at RE off a short working on 4 April 1968.

One of the many RCLs housed at RE, RCL2219 departs to take up the 721 route on 25 May 1967.

A close-up of RCL2221 on 27 March 1971, exchanging its crew opposite RE, which now sports its new 'London Country' emblem. The blanked out LT radiator badge is also a sign of the change. The RCLs had only one more year's operation on the 721, when they were replaced by single-deck RPs, the whole route being abandoned in 1977, which seemed inconceivable in the mid-1960s when the service was well used.

RT3647 turns out of RE into St Andrews Road on its shortest way to Oldchurch Road to take up route 722. RE closed in 1977 on the abandonment of the main 721 route. There was great camaraderie at the garage and drivers still meet every year, occasionally hiring a preserved RCL to run the old route again. Pictured on 10 May 1967.

RT2001 picks up passengers on the 86 route from outside the RE garage forecourt on 17 October 1970. Across the road is Cottons Park.

Romford Golden Lion Crossroads

The centre of Romford at the Golden Lion Hotel with RT908 on a quiet Sunday, 30 June 1968. The bus is exiting North Street on route 247A, which went to OMO in 1972.

RT4298 on route 252 turns from High Street into South Street at the crossroads on 29 May 1967. This route, when I was at school, was worked by single-deck TDs, which I travelled on often as the route terminated, in those days, at Birch Road by playing fields used by our school. This RT is closely followed by an Eastern National FLF – the difference in height is really noticeable.

RT2642 on route 175 at the crossroads on a busier day, 29 May 1967. Again, the RT is followed by an Eastern National FLF – this one on the Southend service, which will be turning sharp left into Market Place. I well remember this service causing a traffic hold-up here when its predecessor, the City Coach Co., used four-wheel steering three-axle Leyland Gnus in the 1950s, it being such a sharp turn here.

Romford Market Place
RT1619 on the 87 route by St Edward's Church on a quiet Sunday 17 March 1968. This was the Market Place, which, on a market day, certainly did not look so peaceful!

Romford North Street

RT3168 on route 66 passes Como Street on 20 July 1967. This RT was one of the Saunders-bodied types, which could be identified by the disused offside route number plate being set midway in its rearmost downstairs panel. Route 66 was converted to OMO in 1972.

A very smart recently repainted RT3861 heads for North Street garage on 24 April 1972. This shot was taken from a position very close to that shown in the previous picture; however, five years have gone by and the changes in the town make for a very different scene.

Romford South Street

A Sunday scene in Romford's main shopping street, now pedestrianised, taken on 17 March 1968. RT4384 on the 247A passes the old Post Office. The lantern-type street lamp that is so prominent here used to be all along London Road.

Romford Station

RT2370 on route 86 already has its destination changed as it prepares to about-turn here on 8 May 1974.

A trio of RTs at the station on 4 March 1971: pictured is the back of RT3861 on the 247A, with RT2770 on the 174, plus an unidentified RT on the 175.

RT4087 on route 252 carries some extra blanking on its radiator. Pictured on 4 March 1971.

RTW62 on learner duties passes Thomas Moy's coal depot on 1 May 1969. Unusually it has been given a grey cantrail and has lost its radiator badge. An RT on route 86 follows.

Romford Oldchurch Road

RT557 on route 103 turns into Oldchurch Road on 11 March 1971. This must have been one of the last RTs on the route, as it was converted to OMO the same month.

Green Line RT3438 on route 722 at the gasworks corner. The small batch of RTs kept for this service were not part of the original number used on the 721 – these had raised metal 'Green Line' motifs between decks, whereas a transfer had to suffice on the 'new' vehicles. Pictured on 10 May 1967.

Green Line RT3656 passes the sign for Oldchurch Hospital on 10 May 1967.

Romford Brentwood Road

RT2396 on the 247A pulls away to turn into South Street on 22 March 1968. This RT seems to have lost its radiator badge, something that would become more prevalent in later years. Note the ambulance of the day and the Manns lorry with a barrel above the cab – and also Hawoods advertising the machine with which we couldn't do without in those days!

Beyond the Brentwood Road turn, RT3696 is in the process of having its blind changed on route 103. Photographed on 22 March 1968.

Romford Roneo Corner

RT4592 on route 193 turns into South Street on its way back to its home garage on 13 May 1970, with another missing radiator badge. Romford station is signed in BR ER Dark Blue, attached to a lamppost.

RF498 on a sunny evening turns into Hornchurch Road, nearing the end of its turn on route 250. Photographed on 17 October 1970.

Romford Heath Park Road

RT3020 passes another RT on route 66 and crosses the bridge on the Upminster branch railway line. This was close to Manor Road, where I used to work at Hall & Co., the coal and builders' merchants. Many a time I had jumped off the bus at this stop, having ensured that I had rung the bell for the request stop. Pictured on 1 November 1969.

Romford Junction Road

Not normally a bus route, Junction Road was used as a diversion route while the new ring road was being built. RF511 is seen here on the 250 route on 5 April 1969, turning into Eastern Road.

RT2396 on the 247A midway along Junction Road on 5 April 1969. Spring came a little late in those days, with no greenery apparent in the trees here.

RT2775 on the 103 has just turned into Junction Road from Main Road on 5 April 1969.

Romford Library

The new Romford, with the ring road forming a roundabout at the library. Pictured on 8 May 1974, RT679 on route 193 heads for Hornchurch.

The view from the Western Road multi-storey car park on 1 June 1977 as RMs run on route 174.

Another high view taken on 1 June 1977, this time showing my old secondary school, St Edwards. RTs still ran on the 193 route such as RT1332, but one of their replacements is pulling out from the bus stop.

Romford Western Road

RT1332 continues on its 193 journey on 1 June 1977. This example still looks presentable with freshly painted wheels. The London Transport fleet name had long since lost its underlining.

Back to 22 March 1971, and RT587 on the 86 route negotiates the roundabout.

Romford Laurie Square

This was at the top end of the Market and here RT802 on the 87 route passes the war memorial gardens. Virtually all was swept away when the ring road was built – at least one of these giant trees survived, as seen in the previous pictures. Photographed on 30 June 1968.

RT3033 on a diverted 66A service runs round Laurie Hall on 5 April 1969 while demolition proceeds. This route was withdrawn a year later, to be replaced by a combination of the new 294 and the existing 66.

Romford Coronation Gardens

RT2221 on the 174 route heads RT4696 on a diverted 103 with another RT following. Photographed on 5 April 1969.

Romford Parkside A12 Roundabout

Modified RF193, at the A12 roundabout, working Green Line route 724. The modifications carried out on these really worked well in my opinion, with the broad light-green waistband helping to reduce the rather high sides of the standard RF and finished with a stainless steel moulding. A surprising touch was the re-introduction of roof route boards, which were used (in rather more sombre colours) on the early Green Line services. The current Romford end of this route is now numbered 712. Pictured on 29 May 1967.

Romford Mawney Road

At the next roundabout west from Parkside, route 252 crossed the A12 into Mawney Road. Here is RT2571 on 10 March 1971, entering the roundabout from the Collier Row direction. The 252 TDs, mentioned previously, worked until 1958 and were then replaced by RTs on an extended route. The next few shots were taken in the last week of RT operation before OMO was introduced.

RT2301 crosses the A12, heading for Romford centre on 10 March 1971.

RT3312 approaches the roundabout from Mawney Road on 10 March 1971. The splendid road signs, such as those shown, are no more. The RT is also passing my parked Imp Californian, owned from 1967 to 1972.

RT4087 passes Mawney Road School on 19 February 1970.

RT2719 almost at the High Street turn, in Mawney Road on 10 March 1971.

Romford Main Road

We come back now to Coronation Gardens; along from here was the steam laundry. RT4347 passes on the 174 route, on 6 June 1970.

Amid the blossom on a fine 25 April 1972, RT2091 on route 87 passes an old roadside pump.

On a wintry 2 April 1968, RT3031 heads for Raphaels Park bridge on route 87.

RT1643 crosses the park bridge on route 87 on 16 March 1968.

Green Line RT999 runs a short Brentwood–Romford 721 working on 26 April 1968. Smartly kept as ever.

Gidea Park

Another RT on the 721 route short working is seen here on 14 April 1969; however, it is, most unusually, a Country-liveried bus in temporary use on the Green Line service. RT837 was to be repainted into Central red a few weeks later so the image here was a rare capture!

RT1782 is opposite the Ship Inn on the 87 route, photographed on 27 July 1967.

Gidea Park Station

RT3033 at the station on the 66A route, pictured on 5 April 1969.

Emerson Park Halt

RT1194 crosses the railway on route 294 and is photographed on 17 October 1970, just three months after the route was introduced. Five months later it would change from RT operation to OMO.

Hornchurch Church
Green Line RT3624 on route 722 passes the church stop on 9 May 1967.

Hornchurch RD Garage
RT2828 turns into the garage from working route 246 on 21 May 1970. This route was converted to OMO in 1972.

RT2778 pulls out set up for route 287 on 3 June 1970. The 287 service was withdrawn six weeks later.

Hornchurch Station

RTs 557 and 2611 at the 66 route terminus on 11 June 1970.

Hornchurch Harrow Lodge Park

Lowbridge RLH73 on its way to RD garage from working route 248 on 21 May 1970, after a heavy spring shower.

The same view in autumn, with RT2571 on route 165, which was more usually worked by RMLs. This photograph was taken on 17 October 1970.

Hornchurch Mungo Park Road

RML2367 passes RT4087 on the 165 route at Mungo Park Road on 17 April 1971. At the time the 165 was the only RML-worked route passing through Romford. The service changed to DMS class in 1973.

Rainham White Post Corner

RT1566 arrives at the 87 route terminus on 6 April 1968. Following up is a Hall & Co. lorry – my employers at the time.

RT1566 backs into the terminus layby. The 87 route shared with the 62 the honour of operating the last RTs in service in April 1979. The terminus shown here ceased to be used in 1974 and the whole route was re-numbered in 2006. Photograph taken on 6 April 1968.

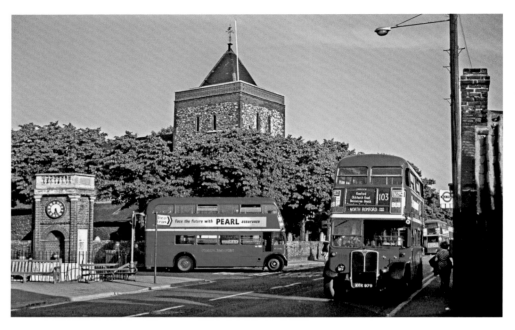

Rainham Church

As well as the 87 that ran through, two other Central red routes terminated here; the 165 and 103. RT2170 on the 103 and RT3486 on a short terminating 87 route appear here, with a green RT in the distance. RTs on the 103 were ousted by SMS types in March 1971. Photographed on 25 June 1970.

RT2938 on the 165 route on 22 March 1971; it would more usually be a RML at this date. Notable is the late use of a capital letter blind, ten years after these were supposed to have been phased out.

Harold Wood Station
RT2089 stops here on route 247A on 6 June 1970.

Harold Hill Faringdon Avenue
RT3554 speeds past (hence the slightly blurred front end!) on route 66A on 16 March 1968.

Harold Hill

RT3861 arrives at the stop on a 174Express – the only Express route (note the blue blinds) in the Romford area. This route was withdrawn in 1977. Photographed on 15 April 1971.

RT3861 again on 15 April 1971, with a nearside view this time.

Harold Hill Straight Road

This image, together with the next, clearly shows the differences between the RM and the RT. They were both photographed virtually in the same spot on route 174 (but a year apart) and are very clean, recently repainted vehicles. This RM, 1429, was captured on 15 April 1971.

The RT referred to in the previous shot is 3861, captured on 24 April 1972.

Collier Row

RT2719 is amid the autumnal trees on route 175, photographed on 12 October 1968.

Upminster

RLHs 73 and 69, with a further RLH disappearing in the distance, are at Upminster crossroads on 12 June 1967. The 248 was the only LT route in Essex requiring lowheight double-deck buses, due to a low railway bridge on the route.

RLH69 emerges to take a different road – one to Hornchurch garage after the morning rush hour on 12 June 1967. Five of the class were kept at Hornchurch for use on the 248 and 248A. This example, oddly as it was always a red bus, sports a Country Bus green radiator badge.

Upminster Station

RT4087, terminating on route 86, passes RLH65 at the station on 12 June 1967. RLH65 was transferred to Dalston garage on July 1969 for use on the last RLH route, the 178, seen earlier in this book.

RLH69 poses at the station on 30 May 1970. This bus was transferred on withdrawal of all the RLHs from Hornchurch in September 1970 to the 178 route in East London to work the last years' service.

A closer look at RT4760 reveals a GB plate affixed to its rear. This RT was one of the buses that travelled abroad promoting LT or London, and they got to keep their GB plates. RT2409 arrives, also terminating on route 86. Photographed on 30 May 1970.

RLH73 arrives at the station on 30 May 1970, with RT4760 in the background.

RLH52 passes the station entrance on 30 May 1970.

Upminster Hall Lane

RLH71 at the terminus of the 248, pictured on 6 May 1967. This bus was the third and final one to go to Dalston in September 1970.

Upminster St Marys Lane

RLH71 has just passed under the low railway bridge, which was the reason why lowbridge buses were required on this route. Pictured on 6 May 1867.

RLH71 returns to pass under the bridge, which carried the Upminster–Grays branch line. It can be seen in this shot how necessary the lowbridge type was. Also pictured on 6 May 1967.

RLH52 'scrapes' under the bridge on 1 November 1969.

Cranham
RLH52 at the 248 route terminus on 6 May 1967.

Corbets Tey
Green Line RT999 arrives on 27 March 1968 at the 722 route terminus.

RT3635 negotiates the turning area at the terminus of Green Line route 722. This photograph was taken on 27 March 1968 with only four months to go before withdrawal of the route.

RLH52 arrives on route 248A. This route had the distinction of being the shortest 'London' service at just over one mile. Pictured on 8 May 1967.

A final portrait of RLH52 at the terminus on 8 May 1967.

RT3276 arrives on route 248A. This route, unlike the main 248, did not have any low bridges and therefore RTs could be used – although RLHs, for some reason, were the norm. Parked at the Horse and Hounds pub is an old Ford car still looking in good condition.

Tylers Common Great Warley

RT4309 comes to grief in the snow, abandoned on 8 February 1969 on route 247 from Brentwood. Waiting, further along the road, was a LT Recovery vehicle for the rescue operation.

Brook Street, nr Brentwood

RT2322 leaves Brentwood behind on route 287, here on the old A12, photographed on 16 March 1968.

Brentwood

LT Central red bus route 287 was the furthest east and here is RT4560 in Brentwood on 6 June 1970, although this was the last year of operation. Green Line route 721 also terminated in Brentwood but, to my regret, I did not record the RCLs on the service here. Such was my antipathy towards the Routemaster at the time that the only RCLs photographed were the few images at my local RE garage. Come the 1980s, my mood had changed and it was the RM family's turn at last!